Introduction

Bad news is so easy to come by these days.

All you have to do is log onto Facebook and you'll be bombarded with stories of murders, kidnappings, and tons of other horrible things.

This is a problem.

Even if you're doing your best to keep a positive mindset, it's very hard to stay upbeat when so many negative things are being hurled at you constantly.

At minimum, bad news can send you into negative thought spirals that last minutes, hours, sometimes even days or weeks.

But if you keep hearing about gloomy things over and over, then you can start to feel fearful of *everything* happening around you. How can you not?

Even if you're somewhat conscious about it, it's *still* hard.

Maybe you don't watch the news or read the paper. I'm not saying you should or shouldn't. It really doesn't matter, because one login to nearly any social media site will still deliver all the gloom you could ever want.

There are endless posts or Trending News articles that will make you feel as though a continuous stream of horrendous things is happening and a new catastrophe is occurring every week.

After being habitually exposed to this level of negativity, how could someone NOT feel like the whole world was crumbling around them?

How could this NOT start to take a toll on your mindset and overall sense of well-being?

It's a crappy, miserable cycle - and one I, and my "positive" friends, had been experiencing ourselves. That's why I wanted to write this short book, which is as much for you as it is for me.

To be clear, my intention with this is certainly not to make light of any of the terrible things that are happening or to advocate for turning a blind eye to injustices or attacks. I believe staying informed is important, *really* important, and I can't stress that enough.

People affected by discrimination, hate crimes, kidnappings, and other horrible circumstances are in real pain. And if there's something I/we can do to help, then we should.

It's a lot easier, however, to get to a point of wanting/being able to help when we're feeling emotionally healthy and have a well-rounded perspective versus feeling fearful and upset.

I believe it's important for people to pay attention to *how* they consume and engage with the news—especially when the news is negative or sensationalized or highly biased and skewed—so they can take charge of their emotions rather than allow their emotions to control them.

Here's a personal example…

One night during the summer of 2016, I had a fantastic conversation with a friend that left me feeling enriched and really happy. We talked for a while and ended our call at around 9pm. Since the phone was in my hand, I figured I'd quickly log into Facebook before winding down for bed.

The first thing I saw was a bunch of news articles about yet another attack (Nice, France).

My happy "quickly check Facebook before bed" mood ended up becoming a negative thought cycle that lasted for hours. I didn't fall asleep until around 2am. And because I didn't go to sleep before 10pm (the "bedtime" I need to function best), I was pretty useless the entire next day.

Negative thoughts are SO easy to come by once the ball gets rolling...

What's going on in the world?
Are all my friends okay?
That could've been me!
Is this going to provoke more attacks?
Should I even travel anymore?
Why are people doing this?
How are the survivors' families coping?
How much more negativity does the world have to go through?

And after these types of big-picture negative thoughts cycle through, it's easy to take that lens and fall even further down the rabbit hole, viewing *everything* as negative...

I wasted my day today.
I'm sick of him or her.
That conversation is going to go horribly tomorrow.
I'm not good enough, I'm not smart enough; I don't deserve to be happy.
Why should I even bother?

Please understand, I'm not trying to turn this into how I was inconvenienced by people being attacked. Obviously the victims, their families, and many more people were about 100000x more impacted than I was by this. It's a terrible, terrible tragedy.

My point, though, is that it's so easy to get lost in these types of pessimistic thoughts. Unless you make a concerted effort to catch yourself and break the cycle, these thoughts can pervade everything.

Fortunately, there are actionable measures you can take to break this cycle, and you will learn more about them in this book.

In the following sections, I am going to discuss a few approaches for how you can better handle bad news and feel as empowered as possible. And while I mostly refer to "bad news" in terms of TV/newspaper and other media news, you can apply many of these concepts to ANY type of thoughts that drag you down.

We're going to cover practical strategies and ways you can shift your mindset. You'll read a variety of things you can do to actively get involved and feel like you're making a difference. Plus, we're going to get real about how dangerous things really are. (You may not realize or believe this, but we're actually living through the safest time in history.)

This book has been written in a short, to-the-point style so you can quickly consume, digest, and apply whatever's most helpful to you. This quote (allegedly from Mark Twain) sums up my feelings around writing thick books for the sake of high word counts:

> *"I didn't have time to write a short letter, so I wrote a long one instead."*

With that said, let's dive in.

Strategy 1: Get The Right Perspective

The information in this section is what I have been most excited to share with you. If you get nothing else out of this book except for what's about to come, I'd be okay with it.

See, I'm about to share some potentially very surprising news with you.

Ready for it?

We're actually living in the most peaceful time in history right now.

That's not a typo, and it's not some advanced mind trick. Even amidst all of the terrorist attacks, hate crimes, and human rights violations - which definitely seem rampant - the world as we know it today is actually a safer, less violent place than at any other point in recorded human history.

It might not feel like it, since we're bombarded with negative news stories. That's because:

a) Sites like Twitter and Facebook give us updates and news in real-time. It's not that terrible tragedies are happening constantly, it's that we're hearing about them more often.

b) Journalists tend to focus on bad news stories. They sell. People have a survival instinct to click on them, because we want to make sure that we're safe and can protect ourselves.

You'll always see more bad news than good news. It makes more money.

c) There's a real phenomenon called "negativity bias." Your brain is wired in such a way that when it's forming memories, you'll remember the negative ones more than the positive ones.

This was helpful when we were evolving. At one point it was important for humans to clearly remember what went wrong so they wouldn't make the same mistakes again, and thus, survive.

It helped us get saved from being eaten by tigers. It still helps us today, actually.

But -- it also makes you more prone to negativity.

It's much easier to remember bad memories than good ones. We can more easily recall times we were upset versus when we were content or satisfied.

The bad news and bad events stick out in your mind, while the fact that there are actually less wars overall is not immediately apparent.

That's why it's very important for you to know the real facts, and to remind yourself of these things the next time you feel like the world is collapsing.

I repeat - we're actually in a GREAT place right now.

By almost any statistical measure, we're doing better than ever before. And while you may think that's not saying much, it does give a reason to feel hopeful. Even if we still have a long way to go, we have made the world a better place than it was before.

Here are a few excerpts from some very telling research:

- A New York Times article says **"2016 was the best year in the history of humanity"**. On any given day, "some 18,000 children who in the past would have died of simple diseases will survive, about 300,000 people will gain electricity and a cool 250,000 will graduate from extreme poverty."

- Another article called "Never forget that we live in the best of times" provides a summary of reasons to be cheerful. During 2016 "the proportion of the world's population living in extreme poverty had fallen below 10% for the first time; global carbon emissions from fossil fuels had failed to rise for the third year running; the death penalty had been ruled illegal in more than half of all countries – and giant pandas had been removed from the endangered species list."

- In "There's never been a safer time to be a kid in America" The Washington Post shows the overall child mortality rate in the United States has literally never been lower. An excerpt: *"In 1935, for instance, there were nearly 450 deaths for every 100,000 children aged 1 to 4. Today, there are fewer than 30 deaths for every 100,000 kids in that age group -- more than a tenfold decrease."*

- The overall crime rate in 2017 is projected to decrease slightly, by 1.8 percent. If this estimate holds, 2017 will have the second-lowest crime rate since 1990.

- 2017 was the safest year in history for commercial airlines, according to industry research.

- The political scientist John Mueller points out, "In most years, bee stings, deer collisions, ignition of nightwear, and other mundane accidents kill more Americans than terrorist attacks."

- This piece, called "The world is not falling apart", shows that trend lines for genocide and other civilian killings point sharply downward. It says, "The world is not falling apart. The kinds of violence to which most people are vulnerable, homicide, rape, battering, child abuse, have been in steady decline in most of the world."

  It also states "Rates of rape or sexual assault and of

violence against intimate partners have been sinking for decades, and are now a quarter or less of their peaks in the past. Far too many of these horrendous crimes still take place, but we should be encouraged by the fact that a heightened concern about violence against women is not futile but has brought about measurable progress, and that continuing this concern can lead to greater progress still."

- Dr. Steven Pinker, Pulitzer prize-winning author and Harvard psychology professor, writes, "in a century that began with 9/11, Iraq, and Darfur, the claim that we are living in an unusually peaceful time may strike you as somewhere between hallucinatory and obscene", but that **"today we may be living in the most peaceful era in our species' existence**."

While the world is far from perfect and we still need to take precautionary measures, it's encouraging to know that the steps we have taken towards creating a safer environment have made a difference.

I'm not saying we should gloss over crime or violence when it occurs. The bad things that still occur are not, in any way, negligible.

It's also nice to know when you're feeling hopeless that everything is not going downhill and in fact, it's getting better. The world has actually become a safer, more tolerant, and respectful place.

In fact, one article written in September 2017 contends that this may be as good as it will ever get. Here's an excerpt:

"Today, we find ourselves in the midst of the Long Peace (no two superpowers have gone to war since World War II), in the wake of the Rights Revolutions (women's rights, gay rights and animal rights), and smack in the middle of the New Peace (the prevalence of organized conflicts, including terrorist attacks, has declined since the end of the Cold War). Meanwhile, the number of democracies

has risen around the world with a corresponding decline in autocracies."

The article goes on to say that in the future we'll likely be impacted by climate change or possibly even interplanetary asteroid wars. And right now, in this moment in time - we have it really, really good.

I remember reading a book written in the early 1900s that talked about how "children today simply don't listen to their parents." It talked about how children were disrespectful, entitled, and not brought up as well as previous generations were.

What we all need to realize is that every generation says the same thing about the subsequent one.

It's very easy for anyone, at any time, to adopt the mindset that things are getting worse.

The facts show this isn't the case, though. Things are improving. There are many great people in the world. And we need to hold onto those truths and that perspective.

Keep this all in mind whenever you start feeling like everything is going to hell in a handbasket.

Strategy 2: How To NOT Close Down, Escape, Or Numb Out

Everything in Strategy 1 is very important. As mentioned, if that perspective is the only thing you get out of this book, you'll be in a powerful place. You can remind yourself of the real facts every time you see something negative.

We're also going to go over other strategies you can use to defend yourself against bad news. Even if you know the stats, it's possible that something could still catch you off guard and start a downward spiral.

In this section, we're going to cover how you can stay emotionally open when you hear bad news.

You can make this mean "bad news" in the media, or you can even apply it to anything unpleasant that happens in your life. We get taken down from "major" things like losing a job, the death of a pet, or receiving bad news about yourself or a loved one… as well as "minor" things like receiving a passive aggressive comment from a boss, having a small fight with your partner, or getting a stressful bill in the mail.

After something bad happens, it's very easy to "cope" by looking for an escape route: we can become numb, shut down, or let the negativity completely consume us to the point where the situation feels utterly hopeless.

As you can probably guess, escapism is not an effective coping technique. Not only does it disconnect us from ourselves and other people, but it leaves us without any resolution or support for our feelings.

The night I heard about the attacks in Nice (as mentioned in the introduction), I felt isolated and detached. It felt like there was nothing that I or anyone else could do that would make a difference. But this type of reaction is not helpful - or accurate, for that matter.

If something gloomy happens and it makes you want to cry, get mad, or worry - let yourself. We *should* feel our feelings. We don't want to become numb or shut down. We just don't want to get *stuck* in our feelings if they're not helpful. And most likely, you'll be able to tell the difference between feelings that are helpful and those that are not.

Getting stuck feeling negative or numb disengages you from the world and prevents you from feeling alive. It's also much harder to be the change you wish to see in the world when you're not fully connected to yourself.

Of course, staying emotionally open is a lot easier said than done. That's why I'm going to go over a few practical things you can do to stay emotionally available after being exposed to unpleasant news.

You can pick and choose which ones work best for you. The more you do, the happier you will be.

1. Breathe deeply

In any type of fear-based situation, your breath will most likely feel shallow and constricted. This can happen whenever you start to feel fearful or anxious about something.

As soon as you see or hear something worrisome, do your best to take full, deep breaths.

Breathing deeply sounds like such a simple and common sense thing to do, but it's not what most of us do when we're upset.

Here's a simple diaphragmatic breathing exercise that you can try:

First, take a few normal breaths.

Then, take a deep breath, counting to four as you slowly inhale through your nose.

Hold your breath for a couple of seconds (no more than six or seven).

Then, exhale slowly through your mouth for a count of four to eight.

Repeat this exercise several times.

Then, try it again while placing one hand on your abdomen, just beneath your belly button.

Feel as your hand rises each time you inhale and falls each time you exhale.

Keep your belly relaxed as you do this so it can expand fully.

It might take you a few moments to access deep breaths. The longer it takes, the more you needed them.

Deep breaths will help you release tension in your body. When your breath is shallow, you aren't getting the amount of oxygen that you need, so your body becomes constricted.

Slowing down to breathe also activates your parasympathetic nervous system. This means you vacate "fight or flight" mode and enter into a more relaxed and rested state, in which more oxygen is flowing through your body, decreasing your tension level.

Breathing deeply also gives you a heightened sense of awareness, as you become more connected to your body and to your intuition. You're able to gain more perspective and access a more emotionally neutral, wiser state of being.

2. Name what's scaring you

Another effective technique is to shine light on what's bothering you via mindfulness. It's an excellent way to retrain your brain and develop more effective coping skills.

Mindfulness is defined as "a technique in which one focuses one's full attention only on the present, experiencing thoughts, feelings, and sensations but not judging them."

Here's a pretty interesting way of putting it:

> *"It's often the attempt to make anxiety go away, not the anxiety itself, that traps us in anxiety disorders."*

It's natural to want to shove bad feelings away and avoid thinking about them at all costs. Certain thoughts and feelings are so painful that we just can't bear to tolerate them or allow them to take up residence - even temporarily - in our systems.

By bringing light to what's causing you panic, you can finally make anxiety truly leave your body.

You allow "bad" thoughts to run their course just like any other thought or piece of mental content. You feel them, acknowledge them, and don't push them away.

Here's how this would look when put into action:

First, you start feeling something unpleasant. Your body might feel tense or on edge, and you start feeling everything you feel when you feel "bad".

Instead of trying to deflect, walk yourself through your feelings and thoughts. This might sound crazy, but try it before you judge it.

A version of this might go like this:

"What am I feeling right now?"

"I'm feeling anxious and scared."

"Cool. Why am I feeling anxious and scared?"

"I'm worried I will be attacked or injured one day. I'm scared for all the people who are getting attacked. It makes me worried about the state of the world."

"That makes sense. Now what am I feeling or thinking?"

"I hate that this is even a thing. Why is there discrimination against people? Why can't we live and let live?"

"Got it. Now what is coming up?"

"I worry we're going to end up in some stupid war."

"Now what is coming up?"

"I don't know what will happen if we end up in a war. How will I survive? What if there's some massive unrest where people go in the streets and kill and steal from each other to survive?"

"Now what is coming up?"

"I don't want to get killed and I don't want to feel scared to go outside."

"Now what is coming up?"

"Well, maybe I'm jumping to conclusions. None of this is happening. Why should I waste time thinking about stuff that isn't happening and robbing me of my current joy?"

""Now what is coming up?"

"I feel better, actually - like the power this had on me has lost its stranglehold a little bit."

"Is there anything else?"

You would continue doing this for as long as you needed. Allow yourself to get all of your thoughts and feelings out in the open so they can be moved through.

It may seem challenging, but as long as you're staying present, you can do it. And you'll feel so much better when you've made it through to the other side - either a place of neutrality, or least, significantly less anxious.

You won't have any more scary overwhelming thoughts you can't pin down, because you've allowed yourself to put everything on the table.

That is VERY helpful.

3. <u>Stay connected to your best self</u>

If you consciously spend time in areas where you are connected to your best self - where you feel the most alive, the most "you" - then it will be easier to cope when other things aren't going so well.

Here are some activities that make most people feel connected and deeply happy:

- Go for a walk
- Spend time in nature
- Write a letter to a friend
- Get away from your computer and other forms of technology

Alternatively, you may have a certain hobby that makes you feel great. Maybe it's knitting, listening to music, or painting. You'll know. And if you don't, two general one-size-fits-all prescriptions are spending time in nature and moving your body in some way.

Life gets in the way sometimes, so it's not always feasible to go for a walk or take a technology break. If you can do it though, do it.

Another exercise you might consider doing is writing a letter to yourself the next time you're in a positive emotional state that you could read later on when you're feeling down or experiencing fear-based thinking.

Use words or examples that you know will relax you and help you get back to a higher version of yourself. Your own words can help you out tremendously. There's a reason that journaling is such an effective coping/mental processing technique.

A letter might look something like this:

Dear Rachel,

I know things suck right now. It's hard to wrap your head around why some people can be so vicious, and having a hard time understanding where they're coming from makes you feel powerless and overwhelmed.

Remember that even though you're hearing about or dealing with terrible things, these are EXCEPTIONS, and not the norm.

And remember - at the same moment there's a stupid senseless death, there are hundreds if not thousands of people who are connecting, making the world happier, and working on solutions.

Think about how many people came together after the Las Vegas shootings. Hundreds of thousands of people volunteered, gave blood, and offered support. You've got to remember this perspective.

Every time you get frustrated with someone personally, remember that everyone is doing the best they can. Walking away now for a little bit can save you a lot of prolonged frustration. Check your ego and be the bigger person.

You can be part of the solution when things are going horribly, by the way. Feeling sorry for yourself isn't going to help anything. You know that.

Don't let this take you into a negative cycle. You know how you felt after you got done speaking in London, like you could conquer anything? Channel that.

Take a few deep breaths. Remember that you can find solutions to anything, have friends rooting for you every step of the way, and put yourself back in control.

You've got this.

Love,
Rachel

I made that a catch-all letter for both bad news AND personal annoyances. You could do the same thing or write two different notes.

The end result is that I'm positive I'll feel better when I'm in a negative place after reading that.

To be ultra-clear, I'm not suggesting that by performing any of the activities above, you'll be able to immediately feel positive and happy. That would be a wonderful end result, but more realistically you should aim to arrive at a place of neutrality.

The goal is for you to be able to address what's going on in the world from a solid emotional state so you can still engage with what's happening but you're not feeling *worse* or going into the loops.

Remember you need to take care of yourself before you can take care of someone else. You know the whole adage about how when you're on an airplane the flight attendants tell you to put on your own oxygen mask before assisting others in the case of an emergency. If you don't take care of yourself first, you put yourself at risk and won't be able to do much good for anyone else.

Don't look at this as being selfish or not caring about other people. In fact, it's the opposite. It's doing what you can because you care deeply about the world and you want to make it better while also protecting, necessarily, your own sense of well-being.

Strategy 3: Practical Tips And Resources You Can Use For Protection

In this section, we're going to go over three of my favorite practical resources and strategies you can use to protect yourself from all of the negativity vying for your attention.

Tip #1: Download News Feed Eradicator

The general approach in this book is not about being ignorant or turning a blind eye to what's going on in the world. It's about being empowered.

Here's a real-world story that will hopefully help put this in perspective.

My boyfriend and I have a practice in our relationship where, if we need to communicate something stressful, we'll ask "Can you be my rock for a minute?"

Being a "rock" means we can say anything we need to say, even if it might be frustrating or stressful to the other person.

We can either say "yes" - we have the emotional capacity to deal with that right now, or "no" - we can revisit the conversation later.

We discovered that neither of us was getting what we needed when I would walk up to him when he was busy and say something like, "Babe, I'm so sick of you leaving your wet towels on the floor. I absolutely hate it. And, by the way, I'm really annoyed about this or that, too."

Doing that caused him to lose his focus. Then, he would get mad because he felt distracted, and our relationship would suffer. It didn't feel good to me either, when he would do something similar with me. We were in a series of lose-lose situations.

By giving each other the opportunity to make space for these types of conversations, we can create the mental bandwidth to fully hear what the other person has to say. When the conversation is over, we can close the issue and go about our day.

I look at going on Facebook (and other sites) very similarly.

When you go on there unguarded you can get distracted, lose focus, and feel upset if you're hit with news you're not emotionally prepared for.

You can't say, "Okay, I'm only going to see and read information that I have enough mental bandwidth to handle." You have no idea what kinds of information you're going to encounter. And Facebook isn't as amenable as romantic partners are when it comes to respecting emotional boundaries.

Unless you've permanently divorced yourself from Facebook and other forms of social media, you're going to see things that affect you. It doesn't matter what kind of mood you start out in; once you encounter bad news, your emotional state can be completely altered.

That's where News Feed Eradicator comes in.

It's a free Chrome extension you can use to block the Facebook news feed from yourself.

After you download it, you will not see a regular news feed or Trending News. You can manually check individual profiles, groups, or pages, but there's no news feed for you to get sucked into.

This helps you ingest news on your own terms—when you're ready and in a solid emotional state.

And since you won't get sucked into negativity, you might even have the wherewithal to post something uplifting for your friends. They could probably use it.

There's a similar tool for Firefox and Safari called "Quiet Facebook".

If YouTube is your "drug" of choice, there's an extension called DF (Distraction Free) YouTube that does something very similar.

Tip #2: Block other distracting websites from yourself

While News Feed Eradicator is specific to Facebook and Chrome, there are other tools you can use to block complete websites from yourself for an amount of time that you specify.

If there are sites that can easily suck you in, you might consider "blocking" them from yourself until you're emotionally open enough to go through them.

Alternatively, you might want to give yourself "x" amount of time - say, 20 minutes on Twitter - before cutting yourself off.

For Mac users, one great free tool for this is SelfControlApp.com. The app lets you set a period of time to block sites for, add specific sites to your blacklist, and click "Start". Until your timer expires, you won't be able to access those sites.

For PC users, the basic (free) version of GetColdTurkey.com does the same thing, or you can pay $25 for advanced features like daily time limits, scheduling, and so on.

For Android users, FocusMe.com/android/ can either block sites completely, time limit them, or limit by launches per day or breaks between launches. Their app is free for Android and they have free options for Mac/PC versions.

For iPhone users, there's an app called Zero Willpower for $1.99 that will block websites on Safari for you.

And if you'd like to give yourself a set amount of time per day to be on certain sites - i.e. "an hour a day on Twitter", you can also check out StayFocusd (a Chrome extension) or LeechBlock (a Firefox and Chrome extension).

If you'd like to get VERY disciplined, there's a free app called K9 Web Protection that will block certain sites and even topics altogether. If you put in a keyword like "news", it will block anything news-related for extended periods of time. You can even give your password to someone else for extra protection.

Tip #3: Discern against "fake news"

When you DO go through the news, remember a few things.

First, if you have a lot of like-minded friends, it's very easy to be in an "echo chamber" where everyone is saying the same thing. As a result, it's easy to have very narrow information bases and to become untrusting of other people's perspectives.

Even worse, we can scoff at and dismiss other people's opinions and lived experiences instead of being respectful and trying to better understand where they're coming from.

You may find it helpful to read information from multiple sources with multiple perspectives, to be able to come to your own conclusions.

Also, remember that a lot of fake news is disseminated through social media. You have to be REALLY careful about the information you take in because in some cases it is intentionally misleading or just outright false.

The spreading of fake news can and does have real-world repercussions. People form opinions, which consequently determine how they vote and perceive different groups of people, based on inaccurate or sensationalized information.

Two things that you can always do before reading an article are…

1. Check the source: If it contains words like "conservative" or "liberal" in the publication's name, then it's most likely highly biased and not trustworthy.

2. If a headline seems outlandish, you can immediately Google keywords about the story to see if you can find corroborating information, and if you can't find any, then don't bother reading the story, as it's probably clickbait and not actual news.

Using these three tips together will help you not get taken down unexpectedly by terrible news, get control to look at things when you're emotionally equipped, and not get swallowed into sensationalist news that isn't true.

Strategy 4: Have A Strong "Maintenance Level" Mindset

Another powerful tool you can cultivate is that of having a strong "maintenance level" mindset.

I use that "maintenance level" phrase specifically, because your mindset can change according to many factors. It's hard to have a strong mindset all the time. But if you have a solid practice of working on your psyche most of the time, when rough things happen, you'll have a more solid base to work from.

Put another way...

If you're normally very grateful for what's going on in your life, when bad things happen, you can be upset, but you'll likely be able to find the beauty in the pain, and bounce back, much faster.

Alternatively, if you let life just happen to you, when bad things happen, it can throw you off kilter.

Having that strong base - that "maintenance level" - will help shield you against being majorly brought down. When you're able to treat each day like a gift, the negativity can be blocked much easier.

See - we don't know what's going to happen to us, right? We can make plans and take precautions, but we have no idea what our future holds - good OR bad.

Instead of dwelling on fear-based thoughts, why not enjoy what you have while you have it?

The reality is - if you were to go to the mall, the movies, a nightclub, or wherever else tomorrow and get killed or injured in some kind of horrible attack, would you want your last twenty-four hours to have been spent dwelling on *what if* scenarios?

The answer is (hopefully) no. And if you allowed yourself to give into every single worry and fear, you would never leave your house. You'd never travel, go shopping, or see a live event. You'd live your life in a cocoon and even then, you're still not completely safe from weather disasters, bombs, robberies, or whatever else could happen.

You just have to live your life, take precautions of course, but learn to let go of your worries as much as you can.

If you're able to read this, you're in a pretty great position. Most of us in more developed countries at least have the option to choose the way we live our lives (for the most part). Even when tons of things are going wrong, we still usually have options. I might also argue that even if your circumstances suck right now, choice could be playing a role in that—choice in terms of your mindset and how you react to your circumstances.

Compared to people in other places, where millions are senselessly dying, living in extreme poverty, or being forced out of their homes… we have a pretty good thing going.

Another way to look at it is through Tony Robbins' quote: "We all get what we tolerate."

When you hear about acts of great injustice or terror, your natural inclination may be to think, "Well, it's not my choice to have that happen." And of course, you're right about that. It's not your choice. But it *is* your choice when it comes to how you respond to those circumstances. You can either step up and help or you can spend your time brooding over how crappy the world is and how bad we all have it.

You can also look at it like...

Treat each day as a gift.
Look for things to be grateful for.

Appreciate the good people in your life.
Appreciate having access to books and information.
Appreciate the ability to think and express yourself freely.

Even when a situation you're in seems bleak, you probably can still find a number of wonderful things to feel grateful for (never underestimate the power of counting your blessings). Practicing gratitude is crucial in terms of maintaining a healthy, positive, and helpful mindset.

Remember that "negativity bias" we talked about earlier? It's always easier to remember the times you were upset than when you were feeling content.

However, by choosing to view each day as a gift, and by being thankful for every good thing, you shift the focus from the negative to the positive in your life. You can help your brain place more emphasis on the happy moments, the times when you feel joyful and safe, the activities that result in contentment.

When you make a conscious effort to focus on the little good things and the gifts in your life, you will wire your brain to understand that those memories are important too. Then more of those good memories and healthy thoughts will become a part of who you are. You can rewire the way you think, and become a person filled with light and love.

You can overcome negativity bias and reframe your thoughts.

I would love to see more people reframe the way they think, switching gears from thoughts like, "I'm scared to leave my house" or "I don't feel safe" to "I'm grateful to be healthy and alive right now," and "I feel happy and safe in this moment."

And speaking of feeling safe, keep telling yourself that you really *are* safe. Unless you are in some sort of extreme situation, the chances are that you really are secure. And so, live in the present moment as much as possible and continue to remind yourself that in the here and now, you can enjoy your time.

Choose to embrace an attitude of gratefulness for all of the good things in your life.

To help this sink in, make the following commitment to yourself: Every day, look for at least 3 things to be grateful for. You might use the Five Minute Journal app which asks you every day to list those things out, plus it helps you shape your day to be great. You may also opt to keep a journal or have a specific ritual. Either way, keep your mind looking for the good in your life and you will find it.

For an additional challenge, do something every day that brings you joy, whether it's something you do for yourself or for someone else. It could literally be anything—whatever makes you feel good. And it's okay if some days it's purely self-indulgent because you are a person in this world and you deserve to be taken care of and treated well too. When you do that thing, savor it. Remind yourself that this, too, is a part of life that you can celebrate.

#100HappyDays

There's a hashtag, #100HappyDays. I've seen it on Instagram and Twitter, where people point out happy things they're doing or that are happening around them every day for 100 days. I love this idea so much and I especially love seeing when participants reach the end of their 100 days and what their reflections are at the end of committing to positivity over a long stretch of time.

Instead of gravitating towards negativity because their subconscious minds were filtering for downbeat things, after 100 days, most participants start to filter for what's good. Then, their overall outlooks on life improve. Using this hashtag is a practical way to re-train your mind to focus on good things, and overcome negativity bias.

Also, in the vein of #100HappyDays, try to treat the negative things going on in your life or in the world around you as opportunities. I don't mean that you should never feel sad, angry, or upset. You should absolutely allow yourself to feel all of those things if they represent your truth, as these types of feelings often indicate that something else is going on. So try to assess your bad feelings and channel them into something positive that will actually make you feel better.

If you feel angry about something, it could mean you'd feel more at ease and fulfilled doing something to help, like signing petitions, calling your state's representatives, or donating money to a cause that you believe in. You'll know you're part of actively changing things.

If you're feeling sad, it could mean that it's time to re-examine your expectations around whatever is causing you to feel down. Sadness comes from missed expectations.
If you have unrealistically high expectations of everything turning out perfectly, reality will probably not measure up to those expectations, and the result will be some level of unhappiness. Know that we live in a flawed world; bad things do happen, but so do good things.

Expect some bad and look for the good.

This way, you won't be quite as surprised or shocked by bad news. It won't be able to catch you off guard and overwhelm you. And by looking for the good, you will begin to see the good things in the world – the good people, the good causes, the good results.

To decide you're going to feel happy no matter what, even if things don't work out the way you want, is no easy feat, however. It takes strength. It takes stamina. But I want you to hold your power. Stay as happy as you possibly can. If happy is inaccessible, go for content, or at least neutral. And continue to light the way for others because your attitude will light up other people, too. They'll just feel it. Then, those people will help other people to feel happy in a pay-it-forward kind of way. And only good things can come from that.

Strategy 5: Make A Difference

We've gone through the other sections first so that we could lay the foundation for making long-lasting change.

We've gone over the real facts - that we're in the most peaceful time in history right now. We've discussed how you can get yourself into a neutral emotional state, practical strategies you can use around the news, and went through how to keep your mindset strong.

We went through these things because being in a solid emotional state will help you be better equipped to do something productive.

The media is actively breeding a culture of paranoia. People are made to feel scared and unsafe, wanting to direct their energy inward (self-preservation) rather than outward (helping others).

If you're operating from a place of fear, you won't be in a solid mental state to make any kind of positive change. You'll be in reactionary or survival mode. Your choices will be based on exaggerated emotions because you won't have a clear head to rationally examine a variety of perspectives and options.

Whether it's making financial contributions, taking a "boots on the ground" approach, or being as positive or light-filled as you can in order to spread that energy to other people, it's the most helpful when you can do it from a place of positivity or at least neutrality.

In this section we'll graduate from talking about ways to prevent yourself from succumbing to fear-based thinking, to discussing concrete ideas and examples of what you can do to actually make a difference.

And of course, it's a process, as everything is. There are going to be times when you simply aren't in a position to do anything to help. That's okay.

A lack of time should definitely not be an excuse though. If you have the time and energy to worry and complain about things, you also have the time and energy to do something positive. So get yourself in a stable emotional state, then spend your newfound time on focusing on finding positive things you can do versus dwelling on all the ways the world is a terrible place.

In this section we'll go over several ways you can get involved. None of these require significant time, money or energy. They just require a desire to do good. Pick the ideas that work for you, then make like Ghandi and be the change you wish to see in the world.

We're about to go over concrete actionable steps you can take to make a difference in the world. While many of these suggestions may seem insignificant, small gestures can have chain reactions. And when more and more people start spreading love and positivity instead of fear and hate, the world improves.

The suggestions below will also help you have some control, even when things feel overwhelming, in making the world a little bit better.

Let's dive in....

Share Love-Based Social Media Posts And Hashtags

When you're bombarded by a ton of negative news, that's when you need positive messages and feedback the most. We all need love—each and every one of us—because fear limits us; love expands us.

That's why, after the 2016 presidential election, I decided to create the following Facebook post:

> "Be the change you wish to see in the world."
> In "honor" of Trump winning, I'm going to commit at least 71 acts of kindness in the next 71 days.

I have chosen 71 because that's the number of days until he is sworn in as president unless electors go faithless.

I will continue to do more after but this feels like a good first step.

#LoveTrumpsHate

And to kick off my acts of kindness, I posted the following update a few days later:

#LoveTrumpsHate update:

1. My sister said the day after Trump won she went to work and found a woman sobbing. The woman is a Mexican immigrant and her husband is here on a work visa. They were terrified that their daughter (currently in college in Mexico) wouldn't ever get the chance to live in USA because of a Trump regime.

I told my sister to relay the message that if the daughter ever needed a work visa I'd make work for her at my fulfillment center (assuming she does well of course).

2. I paid for the person behind me in line. The cashier was excited about it.

3. I got a gas gift card. On the back:

To: whoever finds this

From: anonymous

Message: #LoveTrumpsHate

4. There was a man in line ahead of Don and I asking a lot of questions today before buying an Amtrak ticket.

He wanted to buy a round trip ticket but kept asking about how he could get the cheapest possible ticket, then he ended up saying he'd buy a one way for today and hoped the price would go down for his trip home tomorrow.

When he finally went to pay for that one ticket he didn't have his ID. He had to reserve it and go home for his ID.

As soon as he left I paid for his round trip ticket. The lady at the train station called him to make sure he'd come back.

5. I lent my car to one of the guys at my fulfillment center for a few weeks because his car completely broke down and is now unusable.

#LoveTrumpsHate #WeCanBeTheChange #66More

While I made these posts in response to the 2016 election, my intention was not to be divisive or partisan to any particular political party. I don't care who you voted for. The sentiment behind the posts—wanting to help people, especially those who are scared or hurting—is universally applicable and not based on whose name you checked on the ballot box.

Regardless of who you voted for, you can still make love supercede hate - and that's the main idea here. And as you can see from the second post, acts of kindness don't have to be huge grand gestures. Simply buying the person in line behind you a cup of coffee is sure to brighten that person's day and put a little more love into the world.

Another thing you can do is create uplifting posts or tweets and share positive stories using love-based hashtags.

There was a story about an actress named Leslie Jones who was on the receiving end of a lot of racist commentary on Twitter.

In response, a Twitter user started the hashtag #loveforlesliej. She basically said, "Can we see if we can fill a hashtag full of nice things for @Lesdog" (Leslie Jones' username). And a lot of people did it. It was something small—just 140 characters with the hashtag—but it made a difference by spreading love to combat all the hate.

As mentioned before, if you operate from a positive place, other people will feel it too. They'll feel better and spread it to the people around *them*.

Leslie Jones never should have had to be on the receiving end of such nastiness in the first place, and racism is definitely still a big problem in this country that needs to be addressed. But at least with hashtags and mini-social movements like this one we provide love with a platform to speak out and raise its voice and show that racism and hate are unacceptable.

Another way you can approach this is for every fear-based message you see, you can post something uplifting. If you feel bad or guilty for that, preface it by saying something like, "There's terror in the world. I feel it. I'm saddened by it and I'm going to share something positive because I know it's hard to help when we're operating from such a fear-based place."

Share The "Contrarian" News On Social Media

As the popular Mr. Rogers quote goes, "When I was a boy and I would see scary things in the news, my mother would say to me, 'Look for the helpers. You will always find people who are helping'."

These stories always exist, and they're very refreshing to share if most people are focused on the negative, more divisive aspects of a story. Balance out some of that negativity!

You can find uplifting news and work to spread those headlines around. This is a really tangible way to fight back against the spread of negative news that overwhelms so many people.

For example, as you are probably aware, there have been heated discussions and media coverage concerning the Black Lives Matter movement and blue lives (showing respect and appreciation for law enforcement officials).

But rather than portraying the two groups as adversaries or as one side being right and the other side being wrong, I found a story about police officers and members of the Black Lives Matter movement hosting a cookout together in Wichita, Kansas. The two groups were having fun together, talking, breaking bread, and finding common ground. And as a result, a sense of unity and togetherness was bolstered in the community.

There was another story during a Texas shooting where people, black and white, rushed to cover a stroller while gunfire was going off. There was beautiful humanity going on even in the midst of the chaos.

To find these stories, check out places like https://www.goodnewsnetwork.org/. You can always locate tales of good - and they do make a difference.

Support Important Causes By Signing/Creating Petitions

The first thing you can do is show support for what you believe in (i.e. your opinions, your values, a cause that you feel strongly about) by signing petitions. You can find tons of petitions about a large variety of current events, laws, and movements on Change.org.

A few years back, there was a story in the news about a Playboy model who took a picture of a naked woman in her seventies in the gym, with the intention to body-shame the woman. She put a picture on Snapchat with a caption that read, "If I can't unsee this then you can't either."

The model received a lot of backlash for her actions and some people wanted to make sure the police got wind of the situation, so they created and signed a petition. The model ended up getting in trouble as it's illegal to take a photo of a person and post it like that without the person's consent. She was sentenced to perform 30 days of graffiti removal services and three years' probation.

Spreading awareness and signing petitions like the one above is one way you can help - just by getting the word out and starting conversations.

Another type of petition I've seen a lot involves the inhumane treatment of animals, especially pit bulls. If you're an animal-lover, signing a petition aimed at stopping animal abuse is a super-simple way to get involved and make a difference. It literally takes five seconds to add your name to a good cause.

And if there aren't any existing petitions about a topic or issue you're concerned about, then you can always create one of your own.

Create an account with a site like Change.org (it's free). If you use that site, click where it says "Start a petition." You'll then be prompted to do the following:

- Create a title for your petition
- Assign a decision-maker (whomever can take action on what you're asking, e.g. a board member, senator, state representative, etc.)
- Explain the issue
- Upload a photo or video
- Save and preview

That's it! Your petition will then be up and running and available to start collecting signatures.

Listen And Share Your Opinions In Open-Minded, Civil Ways

The sharing of opinions about controversial topics often leads to contentious debates and arguments. But there are positive ways that you can state your mind.

Even if your opinions are controversial, you can still share them in a way that isn't divisive or morally superior. Undoubtedly, some people won't like what you have to say, and they do have a right to disagree. But no matter what side of a discussion we fall on, we can all be responsible for how we communicate our opinions and how we react to hearing the opinions of others. And a huge part of this involves active listening versus simply waiting for your turn to speak.

Listening is a real skill that many people overlook. Most people take it for granted without really considering whether they truly do a decent job at it.

What a lot of people don't realize is that it's possible to *hear* without *listening*.

Hearing is passive. Unless your ears are plugged, you are constantly hearing. You always hear what people say. But do you really listen to them?

Listening is not passive; it requires active attention and effort on the part of the listener. It is a skill that can be practiced. Here are some of the characteristics of someone who is a good listener.

A good listener focuses on what the other person is saying. When the other person is speaking, she tries to thoroughly understand their point of view and understand things from their perspective. When someone else is speaking, it's natural to expend most of your mental energy thinking about what you are going to say next. A good listener instead uses all her energy to try to understand the other person's viewpoint.

This is the difference between hearing and listening. It's more significant than most people realize, and it can make the difference between frustrating miscommunication and healthy, mutual understanding.

A few years ago, I met a man at Starbucks. He was extremely religious. While I can appreciate religion, it's personally not for me.

He and I were complete strangers, yet we talked for hours about the Bible and all of these other topics about religion. We talked about things I didn't trust about the Bible and he shared his input. It was a completely civil conversation, even though horrific acts of war and violence have occurred over these types of discussions in the past. I listened to his perspectives and actively tried to understand why he thought the way he did. And he returned the favor – he really engaged with what I was saying. He didn't brush aside any of my comments, and he responded thoughtfully to the things I shared. In the end, we exchanged phone numbers.

We truly *listened* to each other, instead of just hearing the words coming out of each other's mouths.

What this interaction showed me was that it's absolutely possible to spread your opinion—even to people who disagree—in a way that comes from clean energy. If that's a way you want to help, do that. The world could really use more people coming together.

Not only can you have discussions with your friends and family members but you can strike up conversations with people you meet in public places, like I did. Some examples of places where you're likely to encounter friendly strangers include parks, coffee shops, community organized events, or while riding public transportation, to name a few.

Obviously, make sure the timing is appropriate, the conversation is mutually engaging, and the other side is receptive. If you can then share - and receive - clean communication without blame or finger-pointing, it can be a great way for both sides to gain understanding.

Become A Mentor

Becoming a mentor is a great opportunity for both you and the people you mentor. It's a great way for you to focus your energy on something positive (versus being taken down by negativity), plus you'll be able to hone your skills, create a legacy, and spend your energy on making someone's world better.

To mentor people, you can look for professional organizations through your employer, reach out to your alma mater, or use a platform like mentoring.org.

Perform Two Minutes of Activism Daily

You may not have the time or means to travel to attend protests, but you can still "show up" for causes people are protesting about by performing what I call "two-minute activism."

<u>Making calls</u>

One of the most effective means of voicing your concerns (or support) for causes that matter is by calling your local or state representatives. I know making phone calls like that is intimidating for a lot of people. But if you really want your words to have an impact, calling is a great approach.

Government officials keep tallies of their constituents who call about issues, and they really do take this into account when making decisions or deciding how to vote on an issue. After all, they have a responsibility to the voters who get to decide whether they should be re-elected! Making phone calls is the most effective way to influence your representatives.

If you feel nervous, try writing down a script of what you want to say and practice reading it out loud beforehand. The more you do this type of thing, the more comfortable you'll start to feel. Also, if you're unsure of what you want to say, you can search online for pre-written scripts. They're definitely out there.

You can find out who your elected officials are by inputting your zip code on https://www.house.gov/representatives/find-your-representative or your state on

https://www.senate.gov/general/contact_information/senators_cfm.c
fm. Once you have your officials' contact information, remember that
you will be speaking to assistants, not the officials themselves,
which should hopefully feel less intimidating.

Let the assistants know you are a constituent, providing your zip
code as proof (there's really no point in calling officials who don't
represent you, as your call won't likely be tallied). Then, clearly state
the issue or legislation you are calling about and whether or not you
support it.

There's also not much point in stating your reasons, as assistants
receive a lot of phone calls and they don't have time to record many
details. It's best to be as clear and concise as possible. It's also
recommended that if they ask if you'd like a response to say no.

Here's a simple script template you can use when making calls:

*"Hello, my name is [your name]. I am a constituent from [your state],
zip code [your zip code]. I don't need a response. I am opposed to /
in favor of [cause or legislation you're calling about] and I strongly
encourage [elected official's name] to please oppose / support this
cause / legislation as well. Thank you for your time and assistance."*

Representatives know they have to listen to their constituents'
concerns. Otherwise, their chances of getting reelected could be
hindered. If you can commit to making one call a day (or even just
one a week), then your efforts can make a difference.

I know this is intimidating to people who don't like talking on the
phone, but those phone calls really add up when there are enough
people making them. It only takes a few minutes, and I promise you
will get more comfortable with it after you have tried it. This is a
terrific way to really make an impact.

Check "Daily Action"

There is a Facebook page called Daily Action - https://www.facebook.com/YourDailyAction/ - which provides an easy, hassle-free way for you to get involved every day. You can sign up for text message alerts from them (see details on their website to sign up). When you do, you will receive a text message just once every day which will link you to a government official whom you can easily call (usually your senator or representative), along with an issue to discuss or bring up.

This means you don't have to worry about looking up phone numbers or figuring out what to say – they simply provide it for you in an easy, accessible way. It's totally possible to make one quick phone call a day, using Daily Action, and it only takes a couple minutes of your time. You can do it every morning while your coffee is brewing, if you want to.

Text RESIST to 50409

This is a really cool service called Resistbot. When you send "RESIST" to the number 50409, it will reply back and text with you. It allows you to send faxes to your representatives in Congress with your message of whatever you want to say. All you have to do is answer the bot's questions and provide your message (see their website for more information).

You can do this as often as you want, and the best part is that it's completely free. The faxes are paid for by donations to Resistbot (and you can certainly donate if you like this service!). This is a fantastic option for people who get anxiety from talking on the phone, and would prefer not to make calls. You can still make a difference by sending daily faxes with Resistbot!

Get Directly Involved in Local Politics

If you really want to get into the thick of things, and you have some time to spare volunteering, you can actually get involved in campaigns going on in your community. You have local officials in addition to those in Washington, so don't overlook these causes closer to home!

If you can find out who your local government officials are, there may be campaigns you can get involved with. Or you can run for office yourself! Many people forget about school boards and town councils, but these local positions are just as crucial as any others. Get involved locally!

Join/Start Organized Community Discussions

Another option is to seek out organized groups in your community where people can talk through or gain different perspectives about trying times. This way, again, you're not ignoring what's going on, but you're accessing a safe space where you can discuss and process your feelings and come up with real solutions.

Even if groups like this don't currently exist in your community, you can always look at neighboring towns or cities. Or, you can create a group yourself. You could pitch it to people by saying if you're feeling scared about this or that and you want to let those feelings out in a safe place, we can set up a time and place to meet and talk.

And maybe the help you offer won't directly affect the people who are experiencing the actual tragedy — maybe you're just helping the people in your community who are feeling scared — but this kind of help holds a lot of value as well, as mindsets tend to be contagious. And so, if you help a group of people to reframe their perspectives and not feel so stuck in fear-based mindsets, then those people will hopefully pay it forward as they engage in conversations with the people in their circles.

This is also beneficial in other ways. Remember what I mentioned concerning the dissemination of fake news on social media and our accounts turning into echo chambers? When people gain perspective and they start approaching problems with a more positive, realistic mindset, a shift can occur with the type of content they both share on social media and choose to follow.

Maybe they start following different media outlets or they seek out more positive stories about people helping and loving one another to share with their friends and family. Then, the echo chamber starts to break down, because a fresh way of looking at things has been introduced.

Write A Letter To Someone Going Through A Tough Time

Write a handwritten letter or send an email of encouragement to someone in your life that is going through a rough time.

A few positive words can lift someone's spirit in a big way, plus it will help you both to remember that we're not in this alone.

Volunteer

So many organizations are looking for helpers. It's just a matter of you figuring out what areas you're really passionate about. Maybe you're an animal-lover and want to volunteer at a shelter or with the Humane Society.

Maybe you love working with kids and want to have a positive impact on the next generation. You might consider volunteering as a tutor at a youth center or becoming a Big Brother or Big Sister.

My assistant has been a Big Sister for almost two years and she said it has been such a fun and rewarding experience. She and her Little Sister get together two or three times a month and do cool things together, like going to the beach, playing tennis, and watching movies.

Pretty much no matter what cause speaks to you, you'll be able to find an organization that supports it and is looking for people willing to donate their time.

To get more ideas and find out about available opportunities, check out https://www.volunteermatch.org.

Make An Environmentally Friendly Decision

In a past podcast, I went over eleven 5-minute activities you could do to make the world a better place.

The list included bringing cloth bags to the grocery store instead of using plastic, consciously switching to e-statements instead of paper bills, bringing in reusable cups if you buy drinks outside of your home, and not using the produce plastic bags when you're at the grocery store.

Each of these things requires minimal effort but helps you do something that is actively either making the world better, or at least not making it worse.

Send Energy

Everything is energy. Send energy to all the people who are hurting, the people spreading the news, and the people in power with the capacity to affect real change. There's so much loving energy that could be put out into the world; it's literally infinite.

If you'd like to learn more about energy work and healing, go here.

Donate Money

Often, giving a monetary donation is the most effective way to help. Of course, not everyone is in a position to do this. Every little bit does help, though. So if you are financially able, or if you can spare even just $5, then this might be a route you'd like to take.

There are always different crowd funding projects for victims whenever an attack or an injustice occurs, ranging from victims of terrorist attacks or gun violence to victims of discrimination or harassment, and those affected by natural disasters.

Before you get your credit card out, you may want to do your homework and check in with charity watchdogs to make sure your donation has the biggest impact possible. You want to ensure that your money is actually going to people in need, and many charities spend most of their money on administrative fees. Search for a good charity that actually gives all (or almost all) donations straight to the people who need it.

Here is a list of some of the highest-rated charities (this list is by no means exhaustive, by the way, and you can find the full list on https://www.charitywatch.org/top-rated-charities):

- Animal Welfare Institute - Washington D.C.
- PetSmart Charities - Phoenix, Arizona
- National Federation for the Blind - Baltimore, Maryland
- Breast Cancer Research Foundation - New York, New York
- Cancer Research Institute - New York, New York
- Prevent Child Abuse America - Chicago, Illinois
- Human Rights Watch - New York, New York
- Fund for Global Human Rights - Washington D.C.
- Earthjustice - San Francisco, California
- Environmental Defense Action Fund - New York, New York
- Partners in Health - Boston, Massachusetts
- American Foundation for Suicide Prevention - New York, New York
- Wounded Warriors Family Support - Omaha, Nebraska
- Homes for Our Troops - Taunton, Massachusetts
- Center for Reproductive Rights - New York, New York
- Global Fund for Women - San Francisco, CA
- Trevor Project - West Hollywood, California
- Children's Defense Fund - Washington D.C.
- Innocence Project - New York, New York
- National Urban League - New York, New York
- Goodwill Industries International - Rockville, Maryland

You can find a reputable charity for whatever cause is on your heart, whether it's animals, environmentalism, or homelessness.

Just ask.

If you're ever stumped on ways to help, you can always just ask— ask online, ask in forums, ask via social media, ask your friends, family, and co-workers. Maybe nothing I've mentioned here resonates with you.

And if that's the case, just reach out to the people in your circles and ask. Find a topic or issue that you feel passionate about and ask, "What can I do to help?" I'm sure you'll find lots of people who can point you in the right direction.

There is No Shortage of Ways to Help

Depending on what your beliefs and capabilities are, there are lots of different options and a huge variety of things you can do to help.

If you have enough time to complain or feel upset, then you have enough time to help. It's simply a matter of making the decision and then committing to follow through.

Closing

One very important thing to consider is that nearly everyone - including those we consider the "worst" people - think that they're doing the right thing.

They're looking at the options they have in front of them and thinking that they are making the correct decision. They believe that out of what has been presented to them, they are making the best choice.

People who commit mass, religiously motivated killings really believe they're acting in the name of their god and doing something necessary, as unbelievably horrific as it might seem to someone with an outside point of view.

I'm saying this because the truth is...

We are all one community.
We are all one ecosystem.
We are all one.
United we stand, divided we fall.

Trying to see different events, even terrible ones, especially those involving terrorism, from other people's perspectives is really helpful at bridging empathy gaps and humanizing *all* of the people involved—even those committing the crimes—which isn't to say that you're condoning acts of violence.

But when we treat people like monsters and vilify their actions without trying to understand their points of view, it becomes significantly more difficult to arrive at peaceful solutions. And instead, the cycle of violence continues.

It's easy to write things off and act morally superior. But a more productive approach is to adopt an attitude of us all being in this together, which I think leads to more good in the world.

The greatest thing that we can do is not to fall into the fear-based thinking. Instead, we need to choose to love as much as possible. Every day is a gift. Appreciate that. And appreciate people, even those you don't necessarily agree with, because we all have to coexist in this world after all. And it's these types of thoughts and actions that bring about change. Decisions made out of fear only breed hate and more fear.

Motivational speaker Gabby Bernstein says, "At times like this we have to reconnect to our oneness regardless of our political views. The world needs a deep healing and that begins on an individual level. We must practice forgiveness, kindness, and compassion."

I really hope the information presented here is able to help you, even just a little bit. I know these are intense topics and it's easy to feel overwhelmed by it all. But hopefully, reading this has given you tools and strategies to help combat negative thinking and make a difference in terms of your mindset and overall sense of well-being.

Thank you for taking the time to read this.

www.ingramcontent.com/pod-product-compliance
Lightning Source LLC
Chambersburg PA
CBHW021338290326
41933CB00038B/968